50 Spirits and Liqueurs Recipes for Home

By: Kelly Johnson

Table of Contents

- Classic Martini
- Margarita
- Mojito
- Old Fashioned
- Negroni
- Manhattan
- Whiskey Sour
- Moscow Mule
- Daiquiri
- Piña Colada
- Cosmopolitan
- Mai Tai
- Sazerac
- Mint Julep
- French 75
- Paloma
- Sidecar
- White Russian
- Sangria
- Irish Coffee
- Caipirinha
- Boulevardier
- Bellini
- Gimlet
- Pisco Sour
- Dark and Stormy
- Irish Car Bomb
- Tom Collins
- Blue Lagoon
- Long Island Iced Tea
- Tequila Sunrise
- Espresso Martini
- Lynchburg Lemonade
- Sex on the Beach
- Whiskey Smash

- Singapore Sling
- White Lady
- Godfather
- Black Russian
- Bloody Mary
- Amaretto Sour
- Aperol Spritz
- Hurricane
- Vodka Gimlet
- Irish Mule
- Dark and Moody
- French Martini
- Grasshopper
- Harvey Wallbanger
- Alabama Slammer

Classic Martini

Ingredients:

- 2 1/2 oz gin or vodka
- 1/2 oz dry vermouth
- Ice cubes
- Lemon twist or olive for garnish

Instructions:

1. Fill a mixing glass or cocktail shaker with ice cubes.
2. Pour the gin or vodka and dry vermouth into the shaker.
3. Stir well until the mixture is chilled.
4. Strain the mixture into a chilled martini glass.
5. Garnish with a lemon twist or olive.
6. Serve and enjoy responsibly!

Note: Some prefer their Martini shaken rather than stirred. Feel free to experiment to find your preferred method.

Margarita

Ingredients:

- 2 oz tequila
- 1 oz triple sec or Cointreau
- 1 oz fresh lime juice
- 1/2 oz simple syrup (optional, adjust to taste)
- Ice cubes
- Salt (for rimming the glass, optional)
- Lime wedge for garnish

Instructions:

1. If desired, rim the edge of a margarita glass with salt. To do this, rub a lime wedge around the rim of the glass, then dip the rim into a plate of salt to coat it.
2. Fill a cocktail shaker with ice cubes.
3. Pour the tequila, triple sec or Cointreau, fresh lime juice, and simple syrup (if using) into the shaker.
4. Shake the mixture well until it's thoroughly chilled.
5. Strain the cocktail into the prepared margarita glass filled with ice.
6. Garnish with a lime wedge.
7. Serve and enjoy your refreshing Margarita!

Note: You can adjust the sweetness of the Margarita by adding more or less simple syrup, depending on your preference. You can also experiment with different types of tequila for unique flavor profiles.

Mojito

Ingredients:

- 2 oz white rum
- 1/2 oz fresh lime juice
- 1/2 oz simple syrup (adjust to taste)
- 6-8 fresh mint leaves
- Soda water (club soda)
- Ice cubes
- Lime wedge and mint sprig for garnish

Instructions:

1. In a sturdy glass or cocktail shaker, muddle the mint leaves and lime juice together gently to release the mint's oils.
2. Add the simple syrup and white rum to the glass or shaker.
3. Fill the glass with ice cubes.
4. Stir or shake well to combine the ingredients and chill the mixture.
5. Strain the mixture into a highball glass filled with ice.
6. Top up with soda water to your taste.
7. Stir gently to mix.
8. Garnish with a lime wedge and a sprig of fresh mint.
9. Serve immediately and enjoy your refreshing Mojito!

Note: You can adjust the sweetness of the Mojito by adding more or less simple syrup, according to your taste preferences. Additionally, you can experiment with variations like using flavored rum or adding fruit (such as strawberries or raspberries) for a twist on the classic recipe.

Old Fashioned

Ingredients:

- 2 oz bourbon or rye whiskey
- 1 sugar cube or 1/2 oz simple syrup
- 2 dashes Angostura bitters
- Orange peel
- Ice cubes

Instructions:

1. In an Old Fashioned glass (also known as a rocks glass), muddle the sugar cube with the bitters until the sugar is dissolved. If using simple syrup, skip this step.
2. Add a few ice cubes to the glass.
3. Pour the bourbon or rye whiskey over the ice.
4. Stir the mixture well to combine and chill.
5. Express the oils from the orange peel over the drink by holding it over the glass and twisting it to release its essence. Optionally, run the peel around the rim of the glass before dropping it in.
6. Give the drink a final stir.
7. Serve and enjoy your classic Old Fashioned!

Note: Some variations of the Old Fashioned include using different types of bitters, such as orange or aromatic bitters, and experimenting with different garnishes like cherry or lemon twist. Adjust the ingredients according to your personal taste preferences.

Negroni

Ingredients:

- 1 oz gin
- 1 oz Campari
- 1 oz sweet vermouth
- Orange peel (for garnish)
- Ice cubes

Instructions:

1. Fill a mixing glass or cocktail shaker with ice cubes.
2. Pour the gin, Campari, and sweet vermouth into the shaker.
3. Stir the mixture well until it's thoroughly chilled.
4. Strain the mixture into a chilled rocks glass filled with ice.
5. Garnish with a twist of orange peel.
6. Serve and enjoy your sophisticated Negroni!

Note: The Negroni is typically served on the rocks, but you can also serve it straight up in a chilled cocktail glass if preferred. Adjust the ratios of gin, Campari, and sweet vermouth according to your taste preferences.

Manhattan

Ingredients:

- 2 oz rye whiskey or bourbon
- 1 oz sweet vermouth
- 2 dashes Angostura bitters
- Maraschino cherry (for garnish)
- Orange peel (optional, for garnish)
- Ice cubes

Instructions:

1. Fill a mixing glass or cocktail shaker with ice cubes.
2. Pour the rye whiskey or bourbon, sweet vermouth, and Angostura bitters into the shaker.
3. Stir the mixture well for about 30 seconds to chill and dilute the drink slightly. If you prefer a stronger cocktail, you can stir less.
4. Strain the mixture into a chilled martini glass or coupe glass.
5. Garnish with a maraschino cherry. Optionally, express the oils from an orange peel over the drink by holding it over the glass and twisting it to release its essence before dropping it in.
6. Serve and enjoy your classic Manhattan!

Note: You can also make a "Perfect Manhattan" by using equal parts of sweet and dry vermouth instead of just sweet vermouth. Adjust the proportions of whiskey to vermouth to suit your taste preferences.

Whiskey Sour

Ingredients:

- 2 oz whiskey (bourbon or rye)
- 3/4 oz fresh lemon juice
- 1/2 oz simple syrup
- Ice cubes
- Lemon wheel or cherry (for garnish)

Instructions:

1. Fill a cocktail shaker with ice cubes.
2. Pour the whiskey, fresh lemon juice, and simple syrup into the shaker.
3. Shake the mixture vigorously for about 10-15 seconds to chill the ingredients and properly mix them.
4. Strain the mixture into a rocks glass filled with ice.
5. Garnish with a lemon wheel or cherry.
6. Serve and enjoy your refreshing Whiskey Sour!

Note: You can adjust the sweetness of the Whiskey Sour by adding more or less simple syrup, according to your taste preferences. Some variations of this cocktail also include adding an egg white for a frothy texture, but this is optional.

Moscow Mule

Ingredients:

- 2 oz vodka
- 1/2 oz fresh lime juice
- Ginger beer
- Ice cubes
- Lime wedge (for garnish)
- Mint sprig (for garnish)

Instructions:

1. Fill a copper mug or highball glass with ice cubes.
2. Pour the vodka and fresh lime juice over the ice.
3. Top up the glass with ginger beer, leaving some space at the top.
4. Stir gently to combine the ingredients.
5. Garnish with a lime wedge and a sprig of fresh mint.
6. Serve and enjoy your crisp and tangy Moscow Mule!

Note: The copper mug is traditional for serving Moscow Mules, as it helps keep the drink extra cold. If you don't have one, you can still enjoy this cocktail in a regular glass. Adjust the proportions of vodka, lime juice, and ginger beer according to your taste preferences.

Daiquiri

Ingredients:

- 2 oz white rum
- 3/4 oz fresh lime juice
- 1/2 oz simple syrup
- Ice cubes

Instructions:

1. Fill a cocktail shaker with ice cubes.
2. Pour the white rum, fresh lime juice, and simple syrup into the shaker.
3. Shake the mixture vigorously for about 10-15 seconds to chill the ingredients and properly mix them.
4. Strain the mixture into a chilled martini glass or coupe glass.
5. Optionally, you can double strain to remove any ice chips.
6. Garnish with a lime wheel or twist.
7. Serve and enjoy your crisp and citrusy Daiquiri!

Note: You can adjust the sweetness of the Daiquiri by adding more or less simple syrup, according to your taste preferences. Additionally, feel free to experiment with different types of rum for variations in flavor.

Piña Colada

Ingredients:

- 2 oz white rum
- 3 oz pineapple juice
- 2 oz coconut cream
- Pineapple wedge (for garnish)
- Maraschino cherry (for garnish)
- Ice cubes

Instructions:

1. Fill a blender with ice cubes.
2. Pour the white rum, pineapple juice, and coconut cream into the blender.
3. Blend the mixture until smooth and creamy.
4. Pour the Piña Colada into a chilled glass.
5. Garnish with a pineapple wedge and a maraschino cherry.
6. Optionally, you can add a cocktail umbrella for extra tropical vibes.
7. Serve immediately and enjoy your delicious and refreshing Piña Colada!

Note: You can adjust the consistency of the Piña Colada by adding more or less ice cubes. If you prefer a lighter version, you can substitute coconut water for coconut cream. Adjust the sweetness by adding more or less pineapple juice or coconut cream, according to your taste preferences.

Cosmopolitan

Ingredients:

- 1 1/2 oz vodka
- 1 oz triple sec
- 1/2 oz fresh lime juice
- 1/2 oz cranberry juice
- Lime twist or wedge (for garnish)
- Ice cubes

Instructions:

1. Fill a cocktail shaker with ice cubes.
2. Pour the vodka, triple sec, fresh lime juice, and cranberry juice into the shaker.
3. Shake the mixture vigorously for about 10-15 seconds to chill the ingredients and properly mix them.
4. Strain the mixture into a chilled martini glass or coupe glass.
5. Garnish with a lime twist or wedge.
6. Serve immediately and enjoy your vibrant and citrusy Cosmopolitan!

Note: You can adjust the sweetness and tartness of the Cosmopolitan by adding more or less cranberry juice and lime juice, according to your taste preferences. Some variations include using flavored vodka or adding a splash of orange juice for a twist on the classic recipe.

Mai Tai

Ingredients:

- 2 oz dark rum
- 1 oz white rum
- 3/4 oz lime juice
- 1/2 oz orange liqueur (such as triple sec or Cointreau)
- 1/4 oz Orgeat syrup
- 1/4 oz simple syrup
- Pineapple spear, cherry, and mint sprig for garnish
- Crushed ice

Instructions:

1. Fill a cocktail shaker with crushed ice.
2. Pour the dark rum, white rum, lime juice, orange liqueur, Orgeat syrup, and simple syrup into the shaker.
3. Shake the mixture vigorously for about 10-15 seconds to chill the ingredients and properly mix them.
4. Fill a glass (traditionally a double old-fashioned glass or tiki mug) with crushed ice.
5. Strain the mixture into the glass over the crushed ice.
6. Garnish with a pineapple spear, cherry, and mint sprig.
7. Serve immediately and enjoy your tropical Mai Tai!

Note: The Mai Tai is a versatile cocktail, and there are many variations of this recipe. Adjust the ingredients and proportions according to your taste preferences. Some variations include using different types of rum or adding additional fruit juices for added complexity.

Sazerac

Ingredients:

- 2 oz rye whiskey
- 1/4 oz absinthe (or substitute with absinthe rinse)
- 1 sugar cube
- 3 dashes Peychaud's bitters
- Lemon peel (for garnish)
- Ice cubes

Instructions:

1. Chill an old-fashioned glass by placing it in the freezer or filling it with ice water.
2. In a separate mixing glass, muddle a sugar cube with Peychaud's bitters until the sugar is dissolved.
3. Add the rye whiskey to the mixing glass with ice cubes.
4. Stir the mixture well for about 30 seconds to chill and properly mix the ingredients.
5. Discard the ice from the chilled old-fashioned glass.
6. Rinse the inside of the glass with absinthe by swirling it around, then pouring out any excess.
7. Strain the whiskey mixture into the absinthe-rinsed glass.
8. Express the oils from a lemon peel over the drink by holding it over the glass and twisting it to release its essence. Optionally, run the peel around the rim of the glass before dropping it in.
9. Serve and enjoy your sophisticated and aromatic Sazerac!

Note: If you don't have absinthe, you can substitute it with an absinthe rinse. Simply add a small amount of absinthe to the glass, swirl it around to coat the interior, then pour out the excess. Adjust the proportions of rye whiskey and sugar according to your taste preferences.

Mint Julep

Ingredients:

- 2 oz bourbon
- 1/2 oz simple syrup
- Fresh mint leaves
- Crushed ice

Instructions:

1. In a julep cup or old-fashioned glass, muddle a few fresh mint leaves with the simple syrup to release the mint's flavor.
2. Fill the glass with crushed ice.
3. Pour the bourbon over the ice.
4. Stir gently to mix the ingredients and chill the drink.
5. Garnish with a sprig of fresh mint.
6. Optionally, you can add a straw for sipping.
7. Serve and enjoy your refreshing Mint Julep!

Note: The key to a good Mint Julep is fresh mint and plenty of crushed ice. You can adjust the sweetness by adding more or less simple syrup, according to your taste preferences. Some variations include using different types of mint or experimenting with flavored syrups for added depth of flavor.

French 75

Ingredients:

- 1 1/2 oz gin
- 3/4 oz fresh lemon juice
- 1/2 oz simple syrup
- Champagne or sparkling wine
- Lemon twist (for garnish)
- Ice cubes

Instructions:

1. Fill a cocktail shaker with ice cubes.
2. Add the gin, fresh lemon juice, and simple syrup to the shaker.
3. Shake the mixture well for about 10-15 seconds to chill the ingredients and properly mix them.
4. Strain the mixture into a champagne flute or coupe glass.
5. Top up the glass with champagne or sparkling wine.
6. Gently stir to combine.
7. Garnish with a lemon twist.
8. Serve immediately and enjoy your elegant French 75!

Note: The French 75 is traditionally served in a champagne flute or coupe glass to showcase its effervescence. Adjust the sweetness of the cocktail by adding more or less simple syrup, according to your taste preferences. You can also experiment with different types of gin to create variations in flavor.

Paloma

Ingredients:

- 2 oz tequila (preferably blanco or reposado)
- 3 oz grapefruit soda (such as Jarritos or Squirt)
- 1/2 oz fresh lime juice
- Pinch of salt
- Lime wedge (for garnish)
- Ice cubes

Instructions:

1. Fill a glass (traditionally a highball glass) with ice cubes.
2. Pour the tequila and fresh lime juice over the ice.
3. Add a pinch of salt to the glass.
4. Top up the glass with grapefruit soda.
5. Stir gently to mix the ingredients.
6. Garnish with a lime wedge.
7. Serve and enjoy your refreshing Paloma!

Note: If you can't find grapefruit soda, you can substitute it with a mixture of fresh grapefruit juice and club soda or tonic water, sweetened to taste with simple syrup or agave nectar. Adjust the proportions of tequila, lime juice, and soda according to your taste preferences.

Sidecar

Ingredients:

- 2 oz cognac or brandy
- 3/4 oz triple sec or Cointreau
- 3/4 oz fresh lemon juice
- Sugar (for rimming, optional)
- Lemon twist (for garnish)
- Ice cubes

Instructions:

1. If desired, rim a chilled cocktail glass with sugar. To do this, rub a lemon wedge around the rim of the glass, then dip the rim into a plate of sugar to coat it.
2. Fill a cocktail shaker with ice cubes.
3. Pour the cognac or brandy, triple sec or Cointreau, and fresh lemon juice into the shaker.
4. Shake the mixture well for about 10-15 seconds to chill the ingredients and properly mix them.
5. Strain the mixture into the prepared cocktail glass.
6. Garnish with a lemon twist.
7. Serve and enjoy your elegant Sidecar!

Note: The Sidecar is traditionally served straight up in a chilled cocktail glass. Adjust the proportions of cognac, triple sec, and lemon juice according to your taste preferences. You can also experiment with different types of brandy or cognac for variations in flavor.

White Russian

Ingredients:

- 2 oz vodka
- 1 oz coffee liqueur (such as Kahlúa)
- 1 oz heavy cream or half-and-half
- Ice cubes

Instructions:

1. Fill an old-fashioned glass (or rocks glass) with ice cubes.
2. Pour the vodka and coffee liqueur over the ice.
3. Stir gently to mix the ingredients.
4. Slowly pour the heavy cream or half-and-half over the back of a spoon into the glass to create a layered effect.
5. Serve and enjoy your rich and creamy White Russian!

Note: You can adjust the ratio of cream to suit your taste preferences. Some variations of the White Russian use milk instead of cream for a lighter version of the cocktail. You can also experiment with flavored vodka or coffee liqueur for different flavor profiles.

Sangria

Ingredients:

- 1 bottle of red wine (such as Tempranillo or Rioja)
- 1/4 cup brandy
- 2 tablespoons orange liqueur (such as triple sec)
- 1/4 cup fresh orange juice
- 1/4 cup fresh lemon juice
- 1/4 cup simple syrup (adjust to taste)
- Sliced oranges, lemons, and any other fruits you like (such as apples, berries, or peaches)
- Sparkling water or lemon-lime soda, chilled (optional)
- Ice cubes

Instructions:

1. In a large pitcher, combine the red wine, brandy, orange liqueur, fresh orange juice, fresh lemon juice, and simple syrup. Stir until well combined.
2. Add sliced oranges, lemons, and any other fruits you're using to the pitcher.
3. Refrigerate the sangria for at least 4 hours, or preferably overnight, to allow the flavors to meld and the fruits to infuse the wine.
4. Before serving, stir the sangria well. Taste and adjust the sweetness by adding more simple syrup if needed.
5. To serve, fill glasses with ice cubes and pour the sangria over the ice. Make sure to include some fruit in each glass.
6. If desired, top up each glass with a splash of sparkling water or lemon-lime soda for some fizz.
7. Garnish with additional fruit slices if desired.
8. Serve and enjoy your delicious and refreshing homemade sangria!

Note: You can customize your sangria by using different types of wine (red, white, or rosé) and fruits according to your taste preferences. Feel free to experiment with different flavor combinations and garnishes.

Irish Coffee

Ingredients:

- 1 bottle of red wine (such as Tempranillo or Rioja)
- 1/4 cup brandy
- 2 tablespoons orange liqueur (such as triple sec)
- 1/4 cup fresh orange juice
- 1/4 cup fresh lemon juice
- 1/4 cup simple syrup (adjust to taste)
- Sliced oranges, lemons, and any other fruits you like (such as apples, berries, or peaches)
- Sparkling water or lemon-lime soda, chilled (optional)
- Ice cubes

Instructions:

1. In a large pitcher, combine the red wine, brandy, orange liqueur, fresh orange juice, fresh lemon juice, and simple syrup. Stir until well combined.
2. Add sliced oranges, lemons, and any other fruits you're using to the pitcher.
3. Refrigerate the sangria for at least 4 hours, or preferably overnight, to allow the flavors to meld and the fruits to infuse the wine.
4. Before serving, stir the sangria well. Taste and adjust the sweetness by adding more simple syrup if needed.
5. To serve, fill glasses with ice cubes and pour the sangria over the ice. Make sure to include some fruit in each glass.
6. If desired, top up each glass with a splash of sparkling water or lemon-lime soda for some fizz.
7. Garnish with additional fruit slices if desired.
8. Serve and enjoy your delicious and refreshing homemade sangria!

Note: You can customize your sangria by using different types of wine (red, white, or rosé) and fruits according to your taste preferences. Feel free to experiment with different flavor combinations and garnishes.

Irish Coffee

Ingredients:

- 1 1/2 oz Irish whiskey
- 1 tsp brown sugar (or to taste)
- Hot brewed coffee (about 4 oz)
- Whipped cream (freshly whipped or canned)
- Ground nutmeg or cocoa powder (for garnish, optional)

Instructions:

1. Start by preheating a heat-resistant glass or mug by filling it with hot water. Let it sit for a minute, then discard the water.
2. Add the brown sugar to the preheated glass.
3. Pour the Irish whiskey over the sugar.
4. Fill the glass with hot brewed coffee, leaving some space at the top.
5. Stir well to dissolve the sugar.
6. Top the coffee with a generous dollop of whipped cream, allowing it to float on top.
7. Optionally, garnish with a sprinkle of ground nutmeg or cocoa powder.
8. Serve immediately and enjoy your comforting Irish Coffee!

Note: For an authentic Irish Coffee, use freshly brewed hot coffee, Irish whiskey (such as Jameson), and freshly whipped cream. You can adjust the sweetness by adding more or less sugar, according to your taste preferences. Be careful not to stir the cream into the coffee, as it's meant to float on top for a visually appealing presentation.

Caipirinha

Ingredients:

- 2 oz cachaça
- 2 teaspoons granulated sugar (adjust to taste)
- 1/2 lime, cut into wedges
- Ice cubes
- Lime wheel or wedge for garnish (optional)

Instructions:

1. Place the lime wedges and sugar into an old-fashioned glass (or a rocks glass).
2. Use a muddler or the back of a spoon to muddle the lime wedges and sugar together, releasing the lime juice and combining it with the sugar.
3. Fill the glass with ice cubes.
4. Pour the cachaça over the ice and lime mixture.
5. Stir well to combine.
6. Optionally, garnish with a lime wheel or wedge.
7. Serve and enjoy your refreshing Caipirinha!

Note: The Caipirinha is traditionally served in an old-fashioned glass with plenty of ice. Adjust the amount of sugar according to your taste preferences. Cachaça is a Brazilian spirit made from sugarcane, and it's essential for an authentic Caipirinha. If you can't find cachaça, you can substitute it with white rum, but keep in mind that the flavor will be slightly different.

Boulevardier

Ingredients:

- 1 1/2 oz bourbon
- 1 oz sweet vermouth
- 1 oz Campari
- Orange twist or cherry for garnish
- Ice cubes

Instructions:

1. Fill a mixing glass or cocktail shaker with ice cubes.
2. Pour the bourbon, sweet vermouth, and Campari into the shaker.
3. Stir the mixture well for about 30 seconds to chill the ingredients and properly mix them.
4. Strain the mixture into a chilled cocktail glass filled with ice.
5. Garnish with an orange twist or a cherry.
6. Serve and enjoy your sophisticated Boulevardier!

Note: The Boulevardier is a versatile cocktail, and you can adjust the proportions of bourbon, sweet vermouth, and Campari according to your taste preferences. You can also experiment with different types of bourbon and vermouth to create variations in flavor.

Bellini

Ingredients:

- 2 oz peach puree or peach nectar
- Prosecco or sparkling wine
- Peach slice or raspberry for garnish (optional)
- Ice cubes (optional)

Instructions:

1. Chill a champagne flute by placing it in the refrigerator or filling it with ice water for a few minutes.
2. Add the peach puree or peach nectar to the chilled flute.
3. Slowly top up the glass with prosecco or sparkling wine.
4. Stir gently to mix the ingredients.
5. Optionally, add ice cubes to the glass to keep the Bellini chilled.
6. Garnish with a slice of peach or a raspberry if desired.
7. Serve immediately and enjoy your refreshing Bellini!

Note: For the peach puree, you can either use store-bought peach puree or make your own by blending ripe peaches until smooth. Adjust the sweetness of the Bellini by adding more or less peach puree, according to your taste preferences. You can also experiment with different fruit purees for variations on the classic recipe.

Gimlet

Ingredients:

- 2 oz gin or vodka
- 3/4 oz fresh lime juice
- 1/2 oz simple syrup
- Lime wheel or twist for garnish
- Ice cubes

Instructions:

1. Fill a cocktail shaker with ice cubes.
2. Pour the gin or vodka, fresh lime juice, and simple syrup into the shaker.
3. Shake the mixture well for about 10-15 seconds to chill the ingredients and properly mix them.
4. Strain the mixture into a chilled martini glass or coupe glass.
5. Garnish with a lime wheel or twist.
6. Optionally, you can serve it over ice in a rocks glass if preferred.
7. Serve and enjoy your crisp and citrusy Gimlet!

Note: The Gimlet is traditionally made with gin, but you can also use vodka if preferred. Adjust the sweetness by adding more or less simple syrup, according to your taste preferences. You can also experiment with flavored syrups or different types of citrus juice for variations on the classic recipe.

Pisco Sour

Ingredients:

- 2 oz pisco (Peruvian grape brandy)
- 1 oz fresh lime juice
- 3/4 oz simple syrup
- 1 egg white
- Angostura bitters (for garnish)
- Ice cubes

Instructions:

1. Fill a cocktail shaker with ice cubes.
2. Add the pisco, fresh lime juice, simple syrup, and egg white to the shaker.
3. Shake the mixture vigorously for about 15-20 seconds to emulsify the egg white and create a frothy texture.
4. Strain the mixture into a chilled rocks glass filled with ice.
5. Optionally, you can dry shake (shake without ice) the ingredients first to further emulsify the egg white, then add ice and shake again.
6. Garnish with a few dashes of Angostura bitters on top of the foam.
7. Serve and enjoy your tangy and frothy Pisco Sour!

Note: Pisco Sour is traditionally made with Peruvian pisco, which has a distinct flavor profile. Adjust the sweetness by adding more or less simple syrup, according to your taste preferences. Some variations include adding a few drops of aromatic bitters to the shaker for added depth of flavor.

Dark and Stormy

Ingredients:

- 2 oz dark rum (such as Gosling's Black Seal)
- 4-6 oz ginger beer
- 1/2 oz fresh lime juice
- Lime wedge for garnish
- Ice cubes

Instructions:

1. Fill a highball glass with ice cubes.
2. Pour the dark rum over the ice.
3. Squeeze the fresh lime juice into the glass.
4. Top up the glass with ginger beer, leaving some space at the top.
5. Stir gently to mix the ingredients.
6. Garnish with a lime wedge.
7. Serve and enjoy your refreshing Dark and Stormy!

Note: The Dark and Stormy is traditionally made with Gosling's Black Seal rum and ginger beer. Adjust the proportions of rum, ginger beer, and lime juice according to your taste preferences. You can also experiment with different types of dark rum for variations in flavor.

Irish Car Bomb

Ingredients:

- 1/2 pint of Irish stout beer (such as Guinness)
- 1/2 shot of Irish cream liqueur (such as Baileys Irish Cream)
- 1/2 shot of Irish whiskey (such as Jameson)
- Optional: whipped cream for topping (optional)

Instructions:

1. Pour the Irish cream liqueur and Irish whiskey into a shot glass.
2. Fill a pint glass halfway with Irish stout beer.
3. Drop the shot glass into the pint glass of beer.
4. Optionally, top the drink with whipped cream.
5. Serve immediately and enjoy your festive Irish Car Bomb!

Note: The name "Irish Car Bomb" has generated controversy due to its reference to a violent act, and some may find it offensive. You may also hear this drink referred to simply as a "Car Bomb." If you're uncomfortable with the name, feel free to refer to it as a "Depth Charge" or simply as the combination of its ingredients. Additionally, please drink responsibly and be aware of the potential dangers associated with consuming alcohol in excess.

Tom Collins

Ingredients:

- 2 oz gin
- 1 oz fresh lemon juice
- 1/2 oz simple syrup
- Club soda
- Lemon slice and cherry for garnish
- Ice cubes

Instructions:

1. Fill a Collins glass (or a highball glass) with ice cubes.
2. In a cocktail shaker, combine the gin, fresh lemon juice, and simple syrup.
3. Add ice to the shaker and shake well for about 10-15 seconds to chill the mixture.
4. Strain the mixture into the prepared Collins glass over the ice.
5. Top up the glass with club soda, leaving some space at the top.
6. Stir gently to mix.
7. Garnish with a lemon slice and a cherry.
8. Optionally, you can add a straw for sipping.
9. Serve and enjoy your refreshing Tom Collins!

Note: The Tom Collins is a versatile cocktail, and you can adjust the sweetness by adding more or less simple syrup, according to your taste preferences. You can also experiment with different types of gin for variations in flavor.

Blue Lagoon

Ingredients:

- 1 1/2 oz vodka
- 1/2 oz blue curaçao
- Lemonade or lemon-lime soda
- Lemon slice or cherry for garnish
- Ice cubes

Instructions:

1. Fill a highball glass with ice cubes.
2. Pour the vodka and blue curaçao into the glass.
3. Top up the glass with lemonade or lemon-lime soda.
4. Stir gently to mix the ingredients and achieve a uniform blue color.
5. Garnish with a lemon slice or a cherry.
6. Optionally, you can add a straw for sipping.
7. Serve and enjoy your vibrant and refreshing Blue Lagoon!

Note: The Blue Lagoon is typically served in a highball glass, but you can also use a hurricane glass for a more festive presentation. Adjust the proportions of vodka, blue curaçao, and lemonade/soda according to your taste preferences. You can also experiment with different garnishes and variations of this cocktail.

Long Island Iced Tea

Ingredients:

- 1/2 oz vodka
- 1/2 oz white rum
- 1/2 oz gin
- 1/2 oz tequila
- 1/2 oz triple sec
- 3/4 oz fresh lemon juice
- 3/4 oz simple syrup
- Cola
- Lemon wedge or slice for garnish
- Ice cubes

Instructions:

1. Fill a cocktail shaker with ice cubes.
2. Add the vodka, white rum, gin, tequila, triple sec, fresh lemon juice, and simple syrup to the shaker.
3. Shake the mixture vigorously for about 10-15 seconds to chill the ingredients and properly mix them.
4. Fill a highball glass with ice cubes.
5. Strain the mixture into the prepared glass.
6. Top up the glass with cola, leaving some space at the top.
7. Stir gently to mix.
8. Garnish with a lemon wedge or slice.
9. Optionally, you can add a straw for sipping.
10. Serve and enjoy your potent and refreshing Long Island Iced Tea!

Note: The Long Island Iced Tea is a strong cocktail, so drink responsibly. Adjust the proportions of spirits and sweetness (simple syrup) according to your taste preferences. Be mindful of the alcohol content, as it can be deceptive due to the combination of spirits and mixers.

Tequila Sunrise

Ingredients:

- 2 oz tequila
- 4 oz orange juice
- 1/2 oz grenadine syrup
- Orange slice and cherry for garnish
- Ice cubes

Instructions:

1. Fill a highball glass with ice cubes.
2. Pour the tequila and orange juice into the glass.
3. Stir gently to mix the ingredients.
4. Slowly pour the grenadine syrup into the glass over the back of a spoon. This will create a gradient effect, with the grenadine sinking to the bottom of the glass.
5. Do not stir after adding the grenadine, to maintain the layered look of the cocktail.
6. Garnish with an orange slice and a cherry.
7. Optionally, you can add a straw for sipping.
8. Serve and enjoy your beautiful Tequila Sunrise!

Note: The Tequila Sunrise is traditionally served in a highball glass to showcase its colorful layers. Adjust the sweetness by adding more or less grenadine syrup, according to your taste preferences. You can also experiment with different types of tequila for variations in flavor.

Espresso Martini

Ingredients:

- 1 1/2 oz vodka
- 1 oz coffee liqueur (such as Kahlúa)
- 1 oz freshly brewed espresso (cooled to room temperature)
- 1/4 oz simple syrup (optional, adjust to taste)
- Coffee beans for garnish (optional)
- Ice cubes

Instructions:

1. Fill a shaker with ice cubes.
2. Pour the vodka, coffee liqueur, and freshly brewed espresso into the shaker.
3. Add simple syrup if desired, depending on your preference for sweetness.
4. Shake the mixture vigorously for about 10-15 seconds to chill the ingredients and properly mix them.
5. Strain the mixture into a chilled martini glass.
6. Optionally, garnish with a few coffee beans on top for a decorative touch.
7. Serve immediately and enjoy your smooth and caffeinated Espresso Martini!

Note: Make sure to cool the espresso to room temperature before adding it to the shaker to prevent dilution from melting ice. Adjust the sweetness by adding more or less simple syrup, according to your taste preferences. You can also experiment with flavored vodka or coffee liqueur for variations on the classic recipe.

Lynchburg Lemonade

Ingredients:

- 1 1/2 oz whiskey (such as Jack Daniel's Tennessee whiskey)
- 1/2 oz triple sec
- 1 oz fresh lemon juice
- 1/2 oz simple syrup
- Lemon-lime soda (such as Sprite or 7UP)
- Lemon slice for garnish
- Ice cubes

Instructions:

1. Fill a Collins glass (or a highball glass) with ice cubes.
2. Pour the whiskey, triple sec, fresh lemon juice, and simple syrup into the glass.
3. Stir gently to mix the ingredients.
4. Top up the glass with lemon-lime soda, leaving some space at the top.
5. Stir again to combine.
6. Garnish with a lemon slice.
7. Optionally, you can add a straw for sipping.
8. Serve and enjoy your refreshing Lynchburg Lemonade!

Note: The Lynchburg Lemonade is traditionally served in a Collins glass with plenty of ice. Adjust the sweetness by adding more or less simple syrup, according to your taste preferences. You can also experiment with different types of whiskey for variations in flavor.

Sex on the Beach

Ingredients:

- 1 1/2 oz vodka
- 1/2 oz peach schnapps
- 2 oz cranberry juice
- 2 oz orange juice
- Orange slice or cherry for garnish
- Ice cubes

Instructions:

1. Fill a cocktail shaker with ice cubes.
2. Add the vodka, peach schnapps, cranberry juice, and orange juice to the shaker.
3. Shake the mixture vigorously for about 10-15 seconds to chill the ingredients and properly mix them.
4. Fill a highball glass with ice cubes.
5. Strain the mixture into the prepared glass.
6. Garnish with an orange slice or a cherry.
7. Optionally, you can add a straw for sipping.
8. Serve and enjoy your tropical and fruity Sex on the Beach!

Note: Sex on the Beach is traditionally served in a highball glass with plenty of ice. Adjust the proportions of vodka, peach schnapps, cranberry juice, and orange juice according to your taste preferences. You can also experiment with different garnishes for variations on the classic recipe.

Whiskey Smash

Ingredients:

- 2 oz whiskey (bourbon or rye)
- 3-4 fresh mint leaves
- 3/4 oz fresh lemon juice
- 1/2 oz simple syrup
- Mint sprig and lemon wedge for garnish
- Ice cubes

Instructions:

1. In a cocktail shaker, gently muddle the fresh mint leaves with the lemon juice and simple syrup.
2. Add the whiskey and fill the shaker with ice cubes.
3. Shake the mixture well for about 10-15 seconds to chill the ingredients.
4. Strain the mixture into a rocks glass filled with ice.
5. Garnish with a mint sprig and a lemon wedge.
6. Optionally, you can add a straw for sipping.
7. Serve and enjoy your refreshing Whiskey Smash!

Note: The Whiskey Smash is a versatile cocktail, and you can adjust the proportions of whiskey, lemon juice, and simple syrup according to your taste preferences. You can also experiment with different types of whiskey for variations in flavor.

Singapore Sling

Ingredients:

- 1 1/2 oz gin
- 1/2 oz cherry liqueur (such as Cherry Heering)
- 1/4 oz Cointreau
- 1/4 oz Benedictine
- 1 oz fresh lime juice
- 1/2 oz grenadine
- 2 oz pineapple juice
- Club soda
- Pineapple slice and cherry for garnish
- Ice cubes

Instructions:

1. Fill a shaker with ice cubes.
2. Add the gin, cherry liqueur, Cointreau, Benedictine, lime juice, grenadine, and pineapple juice to the shaker.
3. Shake the mixture vigorously for about 10-15 seconds to chill the ingredients.
4. Strain the mixture into a Collins glass filled with ice.
5. Top up the glass with club soda.
6. Stir gently to mix.
7. Garnish with a pineapple slice and a cherry.
8. Optionally, you can add a straw for sipping.
9. Serve and enjoy your tropical and colorful Singapore Sling!

Note: The Singapore Sling is traditionally served in a Collins glass with plenty of ice. Adjust the proportions of ingredients according to your taste preferences. You can also experiment with different garnishes for variations on the classic recipe.

White Lady

Ingredients:

- 2 oz gin
- 1 oz triple sec
- 3/4 oz fresh lemon juice
- 1/4 oz simple syrup
- Lemon twist for garnish
- Ice cubes

Instructions:

1. Fill a cocktail shaker with ice cubes.
2. Add the gin, triple sec, fresh lemon juice, and simple syrup to the shaker.
3. Shake the mixture vigorously for about 10-15 seconds to chill the ingredients.
4. Strain the mixture into a chilled martini glass.
5. Garnish with a lemon twist.
6. Optionally, you can add a straw for sipping.
7. Serve and enjoy your smooth and citrusy White Lady!

Note: The White Lady is traditionally served in a martini glass, but you can also serve it on the rocks in an old-fashioned glass if preferred. Adjust the sweetness by adding more or less simple syrup, according to your taste preferences. You can also experiment with different types of gin for variations in flavor.

Godfather

Ingredients:

- 2 oz Scotch whisky
- 1/2 oz amaretto
- Ice cubes

Instructions:

1. Fill a rocks glass with ice cubes.
2. Pour the Scotch whisky and amaretto over the ice.
3. Stir gently to mix the ingredients.
4. Optionally, you can garnish with a lemon twist or orange peel.
5. Serve and enjoy your smooth and robust Godfather cocktail!

Note: The Godfather is traditionally served in a rocks glass with ice, allowing the drink to chill without diluting too quickly. Adjust the proportions of Scotch whisky and amaretto according to your taste preferences. You can also experiment with different types of Scotch whisky for variations in flavor.

Black Russian

Ingredients:

- 2 oz vodka
- 1 oz coffee liqueur (such as Kahlúa)
- Ice cubes

Instructions:

1. Fill an old-fashioned glass (or rocks glass) with ice cubes.
2. Pour the vodka over the ice.
3. Add the coffee liqueur to the glass.
4. Stir gently to mix the ingredients.
5. Optionally, you can garnish with a cherry or orange twist.
6. Serve and enjoy your smooth and rich Black Russian!

Note: The Black Russian is traditionally served in an old-fashioned glass with ice, allowing the drink to chill without diluting too quickly. Adjust the proportions of vodka and coffee liqueur according to your taste preferences. You can also experiment with different types of vodka and coffee liqueur for variations in flavor.

Bloody Mary

Ingredients:

- 1 1/2 oz vodka
- 3 oz tomato juice
- 1/2 oz fresh lemon juice
- Dash of Worcestershire sauce
- Dash of hot sauce (such as Tabasco)
- Pinch of salt and black pepper
- Celery salt (for rimming, optional)
- Celery stalk, lemon wedge, and/or olives for garnish
- Ice cubes

Instructions:

1. If desired, rim a highball glass with celery salt. To do this, rub a lemon wedge around the rim of the glass, then dip the rim into a plate of celery salt to coat it.
2. Fill the glass with ice cubes.
3. Pour the vodka, tomato juice, fresh lemon juice, Worcestershire sauce, hot sauce, salt, and black pepper into the glass.
4. Stir well to mix the ingredients.
5. Garnish with a celery stalk, lemon wedge, and/or olives.
6. Optionally, you can add additional hot sauce or spices for extra heat.
7. Serve and enjoy your savory and spicy Bloody Mary!

Note: The Bloody Mary is a customizable cocktail, so feel free to adjust the proportions of ingredients according to your taste preferences. You can also experiment with different garnishes and additional flavorings such as horseradish or pickle juice.

Amaretto Sour

Ingredients:

- 2 oz amaretto liqueur
- 3/4 oz fresh lemon juice
- 1/2 oz simple syrup
- Lemon slice and cherry for garnish
- Ice cubes

Instructions:

1. Fill a shaker with ice cubes.
2. Add the amaretto liqueur, fresh lemon juice, and simple syrup to the shaker.
3. Shake the mixture vigorously for about 10-15 seconds to chill the ingredients.
4. Strain the mixture into a rocks glass filled with ice.
5. Garnish with a lemon slice and a cherry.
6. Optionally, you can add a straw for sipping.
7. Serve and enjoy your sweet and tangy Amaretto Sour!

Note: The Amaretto Sour is traditionally served in a rocks glass with plenty of ice. Adjust the sweetness by adding more or less simple syrup, according to your taste preferences. You can also experiment with different garnishes for variations on the classic recipe.

Aperol Spritz

Ingredients:

- 2 oz Aperol
- 3 oz Prosecco (or any other sparkling wine)
- Splash of soda water
- Orange slice for garnish
- Ice cubes

Instructions:

1. Fill a wine glass (or a rocks glass) with ice cubes.
2. Pour the Aperol over the ice in the glass.
3. Add the Prosecco to the glass.
4. Top up the glass with a splash of soda water.
5. Stir gently to mix the ingredients.
6. Garnish with an orange slice.
7. Optionally, you can add a straw for sipping.
8. Serve and enjoy your refreshing Aperol Spritz!

Note: The Aperol Spritz is traditionally served in a wine glass with plenty of ice. Adjust the proportions of Aperol, Prosecco, and soda water according to your taste preferences. You can also experiment with different garnishes, such as a lemon twist or a green olive.

Hurricane

Ingredients:

- 2 oz light rum
- 2 oz dark rum
- 1 oz passion fruit juice
- 3/4 oz fresh lime juice
- 1 oz orange juice
- 1/4 oz simple syrup
- 1/4 oz grenadine
- Orange slice and cherry for garnish
- Ice cubes

Instructions:

1. Fill a cocktail shaker with ice cubes.
2. Add the light rum, dark rum, passion fruit juice, fresh lime juice, orange juice, simple syrup, and grenadine to the shaker.
3. Shake the mixture vigorously for about 10-15 seconds to chill the ingredients.
4. Fill a hurricane glass (or any tall glass) with ice cubes.
5. Strain the mixture into the prepared glass.
6. Garnish with an orange slice and a cherry.
7. Optionally, you can add a straw for sipping.
8. Serve and enjoy your vibrant and fruity Hurricane!

Note: The Hurricane is traditionally served in a hurricane glass with plenty of ice. Adjust the sweetness by adding more or less simple syrup, according to your taste preferences. You can also experiment with different types of rum for variations in flavor.

Vodka Gimlet

Ingredients:

- 2 oz vodka
- 3/4 oz fresh lime juice
- 1/2 oz simple syrup
- Lime wheel or twist for garnish
- Ice cubes

Instructions:

1. Fill a cocktail shaker with ice cubes.
2. Add the vodka, fresh lime juice, and simple syrup to the shaker.
3. Shake the mixture vigorously for about 10-15 seconds to chill the ingredients.
4. Strain the mixture into a chilled martini glass or coupe glass.
5. Garnish with a lime wheel or twist.
6. Optionally, you can add a straw for sipping.
7. Serve and enjoy your smooth and citrusy Vodka Gimlet!

Note: The Vodka Gimlet is traditionally served in a martini glass or coupe glass, but you can also serve it on the rocks in an old-fashioned glass if preferred. Adjust the sweetness by adding more or less simple syrup, according to your taste preferences. You can also experiment with flavored vodka or different types of citrus juice for variations on the classic recipe.

Irish Mule

Ingredients:

- 2 oz Irish whiskey
- 4 oz ginger beer
- 1/2 oz fresh lime juice
- Lime wheel or wedge for garnish
- Ice cubes

Instructions:

1. Fill a copper mug (or a highball glass) with ice cubes.
2. Pour the Irish whiskey and fresh lime juice over the ice.
3. Top up the glass with ginger beer.
4. Stir gently to mix the ingredients.
5. Garnish with a lime wheel or wedge.
6. Optionally, you can add a straw for sipping.
7. Serve and enjoy your refreshing Irish Mule!

Note: The Irish Mule is traditionally served in a copper mug, but you can use any glassware you have available. Adjust the proportions of Irish whiskey and ginger beer according to your taste preferences. You can also experiment with different types of ginger beer for variations in flavor.

Dark and Moody

Ingredients:

- 2 oz dark rum
- 1 oz coffee liqueur (such as Kahlúa)
- 1/2 oz simple syrup
- 2 dashes of orange bitters
- Orange twist for garnish
- Ice cubes

Instructions:

1. Fill a mixing glass with ice cubes.
2. Add the dark rum, coffee liqueur, simple syrup, and orange bitters to the mixing glass.
3. Stir well to combine and chill the ingredients.
4. Strain the mixture into a rocks glass filled with ice.
5. Garnish with an orange twist.
6. Serve and enjoy your Dark and Moody cocktail!

Note: The Dark and Moody cocktail is versatile, allowing for adjustments to suit personal taste preferences. You can experiment with different types of dark rum or coffee liqueur for variations in flavor. Adjust the sweetness by adding more or less simple syrup, and feel free to garnish with a different citrus twist if desired.

French Martini

Ingredients:

- 2 oz vodka
- 1/2 oz Chambord (raspberry liqueur)
- 1/2 oz pineapple juice
- Raspberry or lemon twist for garnish
- Ice cubes

Instructions:

1. Fill a cocktail shaker with ice cubes.
2. Add the vodka, Chambord, and pineapple juice to the shaker.
3. Shake the mixture vigorously for about 10-15 seconds to chill the ingredients.
4. Strain the mixture into a chilled martini glass.
5. Garnish with a raspberry or lemon twist.
6. Optionally, you can add a straw for sipping.
7. Serve and enjoy your elegant and flavorful French Martini!

Note: The French Martini is traditionally served in a martini glass, but you can also use a coupe glass if preferred. Adjust the sweetness by adding more or less Chambord or pineapple juice, according to your taste preferences. You can also experiment with different garnishes for variations on the classic recipe.

Grasshopper

Ingredients:

- 3/4 oz green crème de menthe
- 3/4 oz white crème de cacao
- 3/4 oz heavy cream
- Chocolate shavings or mint leaf for garnish (optional)
- Ice cubes

Instructions:

1. Fill a cocktail shaker with ice cubes.
2. Add the green crème de menthe, white crème de cacao, and heavy cream to the shaker.
3. Shake the mixture vigorously for about 10-15 seconds to chill the ingredients.
4. Strain the mixture into a chilled martini glass.
5. Optionally, garnish with chocolate shavings or a mint leaf.
6. Serve and enjoy your creamy and minty Grasshopper!

Note: The Grasshopper is traditionally served in a martini glass, but you can also use a coupe glass or any other glassware you have available. Adjust the proportions of crème de menthe, crème de cacao, and heavy cream according to your taste preferences. You can also experiment with different garnishes for variations on the classic recipe.

Harvey Wallbanger

Ingredients:

- 1 1/2 oz vodka
- 1/2 oz Galliano
- 3 oz orange juice
- Orange slice and cherry for garnish
- Ice cubes

Instructions:

1. Fill a highball glass with ice cubes.
2. Pour the vodka and orange juice into the glass.
3. Stir gently to mix the ingredients.
4. Float the Galliano on top by pouring it over the back of a spoon or by carefully layering it.
5. Garnish with an orange slice and a cherry.
6. Optionally, you can add a straw for sipping.
7. Serve and enjoy your fruity and flavorful Harvey Wallbanger!

Note: The Harvey Wallbanger is traditionally served in a highball glass with plenty of ice. Adjust the proportions of vodka, Galliano, and orange juice according to your taste preferences. You can also experiment with different garnishes for variations on the classic recipe.

Alabama Slammer

Ingredients:

- 1 oz amaretto
- 1 oz Southern Comfort
- 1 oz sloe gin
- 1 oz orange juice
- Orange slice and cherry for garnish
- Ice cubes

Instructions:

1. Fill a cocktail shaker with ice cubes.
2. Add the amaretto, Southern Comfort, sloe gin, and orange juice to the shaker.
3. Shake the mixture vigorously for about 10-15 seconds to chill the ingredients.
4. Strain the mixture into a rocks glass filled with ice.
5. Garnish with an orange slice and a cherry.
6. Optionally, you can add a straw for sipping.
7. Serve and enjoy your fruity and flavorful Alabama Slammer!

Note: The Alabama Slammer is traditionally served in a rocks glass with plenty of ice. Adjust the proportions of amaretto, Southern Comfort, sloe gin, and orange juice according to your taste preferences. You can also experiment with different garnishes for variations on the classic recipe.

www.ingramcontent.com/pod-product-compliance
Lightning Source LLC
LaVergne TN
LVHW081329060526
838201LV00055B/2533